THE MASTER COOKING COURSE

THE MASTER
COOKING COURSE

Craig Claiborne
& Pierre Franey

COWARD, McCANN & GEOGHEGAN   NEW YORK

LIBRARY OF CONGRESS CATALOGING IN PUBLICATION DATA
Claiborne, Craig.
The master cooking course.
1. Cookery. I. Franey, Pierre. II. Title.
TX651.C57 1982   641.5   82-1454
ISBN 0-698-11167-2   AACR2

Designed by Helen Barrow
Printed in the United States of America

Foreword

Over the many years that we have been professionally involved in food preparation—a total of between eighty and ninety years if you include Pierre's apprenticeship in France almost fifty years ago, and my classic training at a Swiss hotel school—we have known that the visual approach to cooking is of inestimable importance where the sharpening and perfecting of talent is concerned. Even the "natural born" talent may need a lesson on how to do the "basics," and being without these skills is a hindrance to releasing creativity in the kitchen.

We have long realized that there are some techniques in cooking that cannot be described in mere words in the ultimate sense. Whether it is the making of puff pastry (which the French call *mille-feuilles* or thousand-leaf pastry), the proper boning of poultry or something as seemingly obvious as how to make a perfect vinaigrette—the stirring, when to add ingredients, and so on—only once the preparations and techniques have been mastered do the meals truly become triumphs.

It is not an exaggeration to say that in our own minds even something as trivial as how to chop an onion or how to mince garlic gains new interest when it is presented in pictures: the physical view of these things in a physical framework is an enormous asset for anyone who wants to perfect his or her techniques to gain total mastery in the kitchen. The pictures thoroughly show—as words do only inadequately—how each procedure actually works.

When we were approached some time ago to produce a book of menus that would detail in print plus photographs all the best and the most basic of techniques for getting from here to there in the kitchen, so to speak, the recipes provided and detailed in this book are what came to mind. We decided particularly to choose one example of a chicken dish made with many vegetables—chicken Portuguese—for this would give us a chance to show visually how to go about cutting a chicken properly if it is to be sautéed, how to cut and chop numerous vegetables, how to cook the foods, and so on. We decided to embrace a number of desserts, including one category which we considered, where the palate is concerned, the most seductive of all: meringues with ice cream and a berry sauce.

We earnestly hope that with this book at hand or at your kitchen elbow you can easily master the most basic—and some of the most advanced—techniques used in all Western cookery.

Cooking is fun only if you feel at home with a skillet or saucepan. And if this volume has added to the perfection of your knowledge of how to go about getting from the beginning to the end of a recipe with a maximum of ease and pleasure, then our effort has been more than worth it.

CRAIG CLAIBORNE & PIERRE FRANEY

Contents

MENU FOUR

DECORATOR TOUCHES

THE MASTER COOKING COURSE

Menu One

Mousse de Poisson
(FISH MOUSSE)

Sauce Bonne Femme
(A CREAM AND MUSHROOM SAUCE)

Poulet Portugaise
(CHICKEN WITH VEGETABLES)

Riz au Beurre
(BUTTERED RICE)

Salade de Laitue
(LETTUCE SALAD)

Meringues Glacées
(MERINGUES WITH ICE CREAM)

FISH MOUSSE WITH SAUCE BONNE FEMME
The finished mousse should have a smooth, creamy texture,
a uniform color and attractive appearance.

Mousse de Poisson
(FISH MOUSSE)

2 pounds fillets of a white, nonoily fish
  such as flounder, sole, yellowtail,
  pike, monkfish or whitefish
Salt to taste, if desired
Freshly ground white pepper to taste
⅛ teaspoon grated nutmeg
1 whole egg
2 cups heavy cream

1. Place the container of a food processor in the refrigerator to chill; or place it briefly in the freezer, but do not let it freeze.

2. Lightly butter the inside of a 9-cup chilled ring mold.

3. Preheat the oven to 375° F.

4. At the center of the head end of each fillet there may be a small bone line. Cut out a small triangular-shaped piece of each fillet to remove this bone.

5. Cut the pieces of fish into 2-inch cubes and place them in the chilled work-bowl of the food processor. Add salt, pepper, the nutmeg and egg and start processing.

6. When the fish mixture is very fine, continue processing while adding the cream in a steady stream.

7. To test the seasoning and firmness of the mousse, bring a small skillet or saucepan of water to the boil. Add a small spoonful of the fish mixture and cook 1 or 2 minutes. Taste the small dumpling and, if necessary, add more salt, pepper or nutmeg to the fish mixture and process briefly.

8. Spoon and scrape the mousse mixture into the prepared ring mold. Smooth over the top.

9. Butter a round of wax paper that will fit exactly over the top of the mousse. An easy way to do this is to take a square of paper and fold it in half, then into quarters. Fold the quarters down, as if you were making a toy airplane, then fold into eighths and so on. Hold the tip of the folded paper to the center of the mold. Measure the paper from the tip at the center to the rim of the mold. Using scissors or a sharp knife, cut off the paper at the point of the outer rim. Then cut off the tip to make a center hole. Open up the round of paper and butter one side. Fit the paper, buttered side down, over the mousse and press so that it covers the top. Cover the mold closely with foil.

10. Place the prepared mold in a skillet or basin of water (to cover an inch or more of the mold) and bring the water to the boil. This is called a water bath or a bain-marie.

11. When the water comes to the boil, place the mousse in its water bath in the preheated oven.

12. Bake the mousse for a total of 45 minutes. Turn the pan in the oven occasionally so that it cooks evenly. Some ovens have "hot spots" or points that are hotter than others. The internal temperature of the cooked mousse should register 140°. Remove from the oven and let

stand briefly. As the mousse stands, the internal temperature will rise to 150°.

13. Remove the mold from the water and wipe the bottom dry. Carefully remove the foil and wax paper. Place a round serving dish over the mold. Quickly invert the mold over and onto the plate. Lift the mold. Use paper toweling to wipe away the liquid that drains from the mousse.

14. Serve with *Sauce Bonne Femme (see recipe)* spooned around and in the center of the mousse. Serve the remaining sauce on the side.

YIELD: Eight or more servings.

Sauce Bonne Femme
(A CREAM AND MUSHROOM SAUCE)

6 *tablespoons butter*
4 *tablespoons flour*
1½ *cups fish broth (see recipe)*
1 *pound mushrooms*
¼ *cup finely chopped shallots*
Salt to taste, if desired
Freshly ground pepper to taste
½ *cup dry white wine*
1 *cup heavy cream*
Juice of half a lemon
¼ *cup finely chopped parsley*

1. Heat 3 tablespoons of butter in a saucepan and add flour. Stir with a wire whisk until blended and bubbling. Add the fish broth, stirring rapidly with the whisk. Cook, stirring, until thickened and smooth. Continue cooking, stirring often, for about 15 minutes. This sauce is called a velouté.

2. Cut the mushrooms into thin slices. There should be about 5 cups.

3. In a skillet, melt 1 tablespoon of butter and add the shallots. Cook, stirring, until the shallots are soft but not brown. Add the mushrooms and cook, stirring, until wilted. Add salt and pepper to taste. Add the wine and bring to the boil. Cook over high heat for about 5 minutes, or until almost all the liquid has evaporated.

4. Add the velouté and let simmer 5 minutes. Add the cream and let simmer 10 minutes. Remove from the heat. Add the lemon juice and swirl in 2 tablespoons of butter. Add the parsley and stir, or add parsley later as a garnish.

YIELD: About 4 cups.

Fumet de Poisson
(FISH BROTH)

1½ *pounds meaty fishbones, preferably*
    with heads on and with gills
    removed
3 *cups water*
1 *cup dry white wine*
½ *cup chopped onion*
½ *cup chopped celery*
1 *bay leaf*
½ *teaspoon thyme*
6 *sprigs fresh parsley*
4 *whole peppercorns*

1. Rinse the fishbones well in cold water and drain. Crack or break them so that they fit in a small kettle or large saucepan.

2. Add the water, wine, onion, celery, bay leaf, thyme, parsley and peppercorns. Do not add salt. Bring to the boil and let simmer for about 20 minutes. Strain through a double thickness of cheesecloth.

YIELD: About 4 cups.

Using a Knife and Chopping Vegetables

When chopping vegetables, it's a good idea to have a portable chopping board. That way you can pick up the board, take it to the sink, and wash it so it's clean again. We also suggest that you peel foods on a piece of wax paper. Then, after you've peeled whatever foods you're working with, you can roll up the wax paper with any peelings or trimmings that are left and throw it away.

The first thing we want to explain is how to hold a knife: The fingers that hold the vegetable should be tucked directly under and the knife blade should slide almost directly against your fingers. Hold the knife firmly by the handle with the other hand, thumb on the blade. As you work, the knife follows the fingers in a smooth up-and-down motion. Quickly move your fingers back and away from the knife blade or else you'll cut your fingers. It may take some time to perfect this technique, but note that the knife goes up and down at the same rate; the speed and distance at which you move the fingers holding the item to be cut determines the thickness of the slices. Practice will make you a master chef, but unless you learn how to correctly chop, dice, mince and slice, you have missed one of the most fundamental skills.

1. The best knife should have a good grip and a nice balance.

A good sharp knife is most important, and we recommend you keep a good edge with a steel or Carborundum sharpener, or that you periodically have your knives sharpened. We prefer a high carbon stainless steel blade because it sharpens to a finer edge, but you may find any stainless steel easy to maintain since it will not rust or discolor.

4. The knife follows the fingers, sliding smoothly up . . .

Chopping an Onion

Now we apply this technique to an onion.

1. First, peel it, then split the onion in half.

2. With the cut side down, split the onion into quarters.

2. Hold the knife firmly by the handle, with the thumb on the blade.

3. Hold vegetable with fingers tucked under; the blade will slide almost directly against your fingers.

5. . . . and then sliding down at the same speed.

6. As you chop, carefully slide the hand holding the vegetable back away from the knife blade.

7. Continue until you have ½ cup of sliced celery.

3. Hold the two quarters together; then you start to chop them. Be sure to slide your fingers away from the knife as you slice.

4. Slice to the desired thickness by controlling the movement of the fingers that hold the onion in place.

Since we want the onion coarsely chopped, the pieces should be relatively large.

15

Preparing the Fish Broth

This fish broth is the essence of almost every fish sauce known in French cooking.

1. You can use just the bones, but they should be fairly meaty, and with the fins. You don't want the gills.

Preparing the Fish Mousse Mixture

In making fish mousse, you can select from a variety of fish. Ideally it should be a white, nonoily fish such as pike or monkfish, and very fresh. The fish should never have been frozen because, if it has, it will lose its protein once it's cooked. It will also not cook properly and will start to bleed when the fish is being cooked.

When preparing this recipe, the fish should be very, very cold.

2. Place the fishbones in a saucepan. Add ½ cup of coarsely chopped celery; ½ cup coarsely chopped onion; 4 whole peppercorns; ½ teaspoon dried thyme; 3 cups of clear, pure water; 1 cup of very good dry white wine; a bay leaf and 6 sprigs of fresh, whole parsley. Let it all simmer for exactly 20 minutes.

3. Strain the fish broth. You'll need about 3 cups for this recipe; anything left over can be frozen.

1. At the center of the head end of each fillet there may be a small bone line.

2. Cut on either side of this bone line.

3. You'll wind up with a small, triangular-shaped piece, which you discard.

4. Sometimes the fishermen, when they make a fillet, leave some bone on the side.

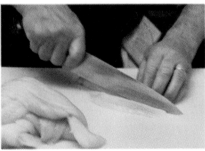

5. Now cut the fish fillet lengthwise down the center.

6. Then cut the halves into pieces about 2 inches square.

Processing the Fish Mixture

1. Chill the container of your food processor thoroughly; it should be very cold.

2. Add the cubed fish to the processor; add salt to taste, and freshly ground white pepper (black pepper grains would be visible).

3. Next, add 1 egg and ⅛ teaspoon grated nutmeg. Freshly ground nutmeg has much more flavor than canned.

4. Process the fish until it's very fine. Here the fish is too coarse and must be processed more.

8. To test the mousse before cooking, drop a spoonful of it into a pan of gently boiling water.

Molding the Mousse

1. Coat a chilled, 9-cup ring mold with melted butter. We like to use a brush.

5. Stop the processor a few times and stir down the mixture to ensure that all the meat reaches the blade and will be evenly ground.

6. When it is very fine, add the cream in a steady stream through the feed tube. The cream must be well chilled and the fish churning.

7. Once the cream is blended in, stop and stir it down again. Continue processing until it is very fine, and as smooth as custard.

9. Cook it a minute or so, until it firms up, then taste for texture and seasoning. Correct as needed.

2. When the mousse has reached its proper texture, use a spatula and scrape it into the mold.

3. This should be pressed down firmly with the rubber spatula.

4. Fill the mold to about an inch below the rim, and smooth down the surface with the spatula.

19

Making a Wax-Paper Round

You'll need a round of wax paper to fit almost exactly on top of the mousse.

1. Take a square of wax paper; fold it in half, then into quarters.

2. Fold the quarters down, as if you were making a paper airplane.

3. Continue folding the wax paper until it's very small.

7. Butter one side of the wax paper.

8. Apply the buttered side directly onto the mousse.

Baking the Mousse

4. Hold the tip to the center of the mold and measure to the outside rim, then cut the end at the rim.

5. Cut a small portion from the tip of the wax paper. You can use either a knife or a pair of scissors.

6. When you open the wax paper, you should now have a wax-paper ring that will fit over the mousse.

9. Press the paper down with your fingers to make certain it's in contact with the mousse and approximately 1 inch below the rim.

10. Now cover the entire mold with a square of aluminum foil; press the sides to make it more or less hermetically sealed.

1. Place the mold in the center of a skillet and add enough water to cover an inch or more of the mold.

2. Put the skillet on the stove and bring the water to the boil. This procedure of baking food in a basin of boiling or simmering water is called a bain-marie or water bath. We use this technique so that the dish will cook subtly and will not curdle or separate once it's removed from the oven.

3. After the water has come to the boil, take the dish in its water bath and put it in an oven that's been preheated to 375° F. Set it in the center of the oven and let it bake for 45 minutes.

Preparing Sauce Bonne Femme

This excellent sauce is made by combining a velouté or basic white sauce with fresh mushrooms and cream, and is flavored with shallots, parsley and wine. Since this sauce is to be served with fish mousse, we're going to use a fish broth as the stock. However, you could vary the basic ingredients slightly to accompany poultry, beef, or eggs and vegetables.

The Velouté

1. Begin by melting 3 tablespoons of butter in a saucepan over low heat. Watch it carefully; you don't want it to foam or color.

2. Add 1½ tablespoons of liquid and 4 tablespoons of flour. This mixture of melted butter and flour is called a roux, and is the basis of nearly every French sauce.

4. Add the rest of the 1½ cups of fish broth.

Mincing Shallots

You'll need about ¼ cup of minced shallots for the sauce. Peel the shallots and

1. Hold them facing you and slice straight down lengthwise about ⅛ inch. Do not cut entirely through.

2. Then turn the shallots and, holding the knife flat, cut horizontal slices about ⅛ inch apart.

3. Finally, cut across the shallots. The result should be small, minced pieces.

3. As you stir the mixture constantly with a wire whisk, a smooth, thick mass will develop. This mass may be cooked for several minutes without browning.

5. Whisk rapidly to prevent the sauce from getting lumpy.

place them on a flat surface.

4. For even finer pieces, hold the tip of the blade in place with the middle 3 fingers of your left hand.

5. Hold the handle in your right hand and chop up and down in an arc, using the left hand as a pivot. Chop from the outside toward the center.

6. Keep heaping the shallots and push the mass backwards and forwards toward a specific center place.

Sauce Bonne Femme (continued)

Slicing Mushrooms and Mincing Parsley

1. Take a pound of washed, drained mushrooms and slice them one at a time with a very sharp chef's knife.

2. Hold the mushrooms on their sides and slice down in intervals from ⅛ to ¼ of an inch. You'll need 5 cups of sliced mushrooms.

Finishing the Sauce

1. In a saucepan, melt 1 tablespoon butter and add the shallots. Cook, stirring constantly, until shallots have lost their raw taste. Add the mushrooms and ½ cup dry white wine.

Unmolding the Mousse

1. There will be some liquid accumulation around the mousse. Pour this off, and discard.

2. Then invert a round serving platter or a dish on top of the mousse.

1. To mince parsley: Take clusters of parsley; tear out the stems and discard them.

2. Take the parsley clusters and gather them in a tight bundle with your fingers and chop coarsely.

3. Heap them and, with the same up-and-down pivoting technique you used for the shallots, chop toward the center, backwards and forwards, until finely minced.

2. Cook over very high heat, stirring constantly, until almost all liquid has evaporated. When you tilt the pan, there should be only a tablespoon or so of liquid.

3. Add the velouté and whisk the two mixtures until well blended. Add 1 cup heavy cream; simmer 10 minutes. Remove from heat and swirl in the juice of half a lemon and 2 tablespoons butter, Put sauce aside.

3. Quickly invert the mold over and onto the platter. Center the mold and lift up.

4. Spoon some sauce into the center of the mousse; dribble a little bit on the sides. Neatly wipe the sides of the serving platter and sprinkle with finely chopped parsley. Spoon the remaining sauce into a sauceboat, to be served on the side.

POULET PORTUGAISE ET RIZ AU BEURRE
A very colorful and flavorful chicken dish,
Poulet Portugaise is made with onions, peppers and herbs in a
tomato and wine sauce. A buttered rice is served on the side.

Poulet Portugaise
(CHICKEN WITH VEGETABLES)

one 3¼-pound chicken, cut into serving
    pieces
Salt to taste, if desired
Freshly ground pepper to taste
2 tablespoons olive oil
2 medium-size onions, peeled and
    coarsely chopped, about 2 cups
2 tablespoons finely minced garlic
1 dried, hot red pepper (optional)
6 sweet (red or green) peppers, cored,
    seeded and cut into ½-inch strips,
    about 4 cups
1 bay leaf
½ teaspoon dried thyme
1 tablespoon loosely packed stem saffron
    (optional)
½ cup dry white wine
1½ cups peeled, chopped, fresh red ripe
    tomatoes, or use imported canned
    tomatoes
¼ cup tomato paste
¼ cup finely chopped parsley

1. Sprinkle the chicken with salt and pepper.

2. Heat the oil in a heavy skillet large enough to hold the chicken in 1 layer. When the oil is quite hot but not smoking, add the chicken pieces, skin side down. Cook over moderately high heat until nicely browned on one side, about 5 minutes.

3. Turn the pieces and cook another 5 minutes, or until browned on the second side.

4. Add the onions, garlic and hot red pepper. Cook briefly, stirring, and add the sweet peppers, bay leaf, thyme and saffron. Stir to blend the ingredients well. Cook about 5 minutes and add the wine, tomatoes and tomato paste.

5. Bring to the boil. Cook about 20 minutes. If sauce seems too thin, reduce over high heat for about 5 minutes or less. Discard the hot red pepper and serve sprinkled with chopped parsley.

YIELD: Four servings.

Disjointing a Chicken

The method we demonstrate here is ideal for sautées or stews because it produces the maximum number of pieces.

1. Begin by removing all visible fat from the interior of the chicken.

2. Cut off the wing tips and the first wing joint of the bird.

3. Then cut the second wing joint. That way, you get more meat and more servings.

7. Continue slicing until the entire joint can be removed.

8. Insert the knife at the tip of the joint where there is a straight line of fat to guide you.

9. Continue cutting through and pull it off. Now repeat this procedure on the other thigh and leg bone.

13. Press down on the chicken with the knife, and pull the wing to remove the meat.

14. Cut through the bones in the center cavity of the chicken; you may want to use a heavier knife.

4. Pull the thigh gently away from the body and cut down, away from the joint.

5. As you continue, pull the thigh away from the body and cut directly into the bottom joint.

6. Make sure to follow the bone, so you don't lose what we call the "oyster."

10. Draw a straight line with the knife from the main wing joint to the bottom pointed tip of the breast.

11. As you pull back the wing, you will find the joint where the wing is attached to the body.

12. Pull back and continue to cut through the wing joint; some of the breast meat should remain on the wing.

15. Cut away and discard fat and skin surrounding bony carcass.

16. Cut the bony carcass in half.

17. Then cut the breast crosswise in half, which is to say at midpoint at the center of the breast.

Preparing Chicken Portugaise

Cooking the chicken will be easier if you prepare the vegetables in advance. Thus, coarsely chop 2 cups of onions. Coarsely chop 6 red or green sweet peppers into ½-inch strips. Then prepare the garlic as follows.

1. Here, we show you how to chop garlic. Your piece of garlic may have a green sprout, which you want to remove because it will give a bitter flavor.

Cooking the Chicken

1. In a heavy skillet, add 2 tablespoons of olive oil. Using olive oil is very Portuguese. Arrange the chicken parts, skin side down, in 1 layer. Add the dark meat first, then the white pieces. Cook over high heat until golden brown. Turn and repeat.

2. Add the onions, garlic, 1 dried red pepper, the bay leaf, ½ teaspoon of thyme, the tablespoon of saffron and sweet pepper. Blend and cook briefly. Add the wine, tomatoes and tomato paste.

30

2. The best way to remove this is to cut the garlic clove in half, then remove the sprout.

3. Chop the garlic coarsely; never squash it with the flat blade of the knife. When you squash it or flatten it sharply, it changes the flavor of the garlic because most of the oil disappears.

4. Continue chopping until the garlic is finely minced.

3. Stir briefly and, if it's available and you wish to use it, add a tablespoon of loosely packed saffron. The saffron is optional, but it adds greatly to the flavor and color of the dish. Stir and cook uncovered for 20 minutes.

4. Arrange the chicken pieces on a warm platter and spoon the peppers and sauce over them.

Riz au Beurre
(BUTTERED RICE)

2 tablespoons butter
¼ cup finely chopped onion
1 cup long-grain rice
1½ cups chicken broth or water
1 bay leaf
2 sprigs fresh parsley
Salt to taste, if desired
A dash of Tabasco sauce

1. Melt 1 tablespoon of the butter in a saucepan with a tight-fitting lid. Add the onion and cook, stirring, about 2 minutes.

2. Add the rice and stir to coat with the butter and onion. Add the broth, bay leaf, parsley and salt and bring to the boil. Add the Tabasco. Cover tightly. Let simmer for exactly 17 minutes over a low flame.

3. Uncover and remove the bay leaf and parsley. Remove from the stove and stir in the remaining tablespoon of butter and serve.

YIELD: Four servings.

Preparing the Rice

We've noticed that most commercial packagers of rice don't know how to cook their own product. Most of them have the proportion of water to rice completely wrong. A good rule of thumb is to use 1½ cups of liquid for each cup of rice. It takes exactly 17 minutes to cook, either on top of the stove or in the oven. If you use the oven, preheat it to 400° F.

1. Start with a tablespoon of butter in a saucepan. The saucepan should have a heavy, tight-fitting lid.

2. Add ¼ cup of finely minced, chopped onions and stir well. The onions should not brown—that's very important.
3. Now add a cup of long-grain rice and stir it well, in order that every grain be covered with butter. Then add 1½ cups of liquid—it could be water, but since this is to go with chicken, we'll add 1½ cups of chicken broth.
4. Add a bay leaf, a couple of sprigs of parsley, a dash of salt, if desired, and Tabasco, and bring everything to the boil.

5. Cover and simmer on a very low flame. Incidentally, you should never "peek" at the rice while cooking; that allows the steam to . . .

. . . escape and it will not cook properly.

6. When the rice has cooked exactly 17 minutes, remove the parsley and bay leaf. Now it's time to take the rice off the stove to prepare for molding.

7. Add a tablespoon of butter and stir with a fork.

8. Next, take a mold—it can be a regular mold or a bowl, any vessel that is large enough to hold the rice compactly so the rice . . .

. . . comes all the way up to and level with the top. Pack it into the mold and press it down well with either your hand or a spatula. An easy way to do this is to put a double sheet of wax paper over the rice and press it with your palm.

9. Place a serving dish over the mold and invert the rice onto it. If you're not going to serve the rice immediately, let the mold sit on top of the rice until serving.

LETTUCE SALAD WITH SAUCE VINAIGRETTE
For a quick and tasteful salad, top an assortment of crisp lettuce
with a simple oil and vinegar dressing,
using chopped, fresh parsley for seasoning.

Sauce Vinaigrette

1 *tablespoon prepared mustard, prefer-*
  ably imported
2 *tablespoons red wine vinegar*
Salt to taste, if desired
Freshly ground pepper to taste
½ *cup corn, vegetable, peanut or olive*
  oil
2 *tablespoons chopped parsley*

1. Put the mustard and vinegar in a small mixing bowl. Add salt and pepper to taste.

2. Start beating vigorously with a wire whisk. Gradually beat in the oil.

3. Whisk in the chopped parsley.

YIELD: About ¾ of a cup.

Preparing Sauce Vinaigrette

The simplest oil and vinegar dressing for four people is 1 tablespoon of prepared mustard (preferably Dijon), salt, pepper and 2 tablespoons of red wine vinegar.

1. Combine all of these ingredients in a bowl and whisk gradually.

2. Add ½ cup of corn oil, or you can use peanut, vegetable or olive oil.

3. To this add 2 heaping tablespoons of chopped parsley. With a vinegar dressing, you can add almost any sweet herbs or seasoning, such as chopped shallots, basil, dill, scallions, finely chopped onions, and so on. There are many variations.

4. Just mix very well, until all the ingredients are homogenized and the texture is even.

MERINGUES GLACÉES
Place a scoop of the best vanilla ice cream on a plate
between two meringues, and top with raspberry purée.

Meringues Glacées
(M E R I N G U E S W I T H I C E C R E A M)

MERINGUES

1 *tablespoon flour*
3 *large eggs*
¾ *cup very fine sugar*

1. Preheat the oven to 200° F.
2. Using a pastry brush, lightly butter the surface of 1 or 2 baking sheets. Add about a tablespoon of flour and shake the baking sheet so that the flour coats the surface evenly.
3. Separate the egg whites from the yolks. There should be about ½ cup of whites. Reserve the yolks for another use.
4. Using an electric beater, beat the whites on low speed until they start to foam. Gradually increase the speed to high. Add the sugar, a little at a time. Continue beating until the meringue is quite stiff and glossy in appearance.
5. Outfit a pastry bag with a round No. 7 pastry tube. Fill the bag with the meringue.
6. Lift the bag from the top and shake it up and down gently to make the meringue compact inside the bag. Twist the top of the bag and hold the twist in your right hand; hold the tube between the thumb and forefinger. Put the bottom of the tube on the buttered and floured baking sheet and press out the meringue mixture into ovals or rounds.
7. Place the baking sheets in the oven and bake for about 2 hours.
YIELD: About 14 meringues.

RASPBERRY SAUCE

3 *cups red, ripe, firm raspberries, or two*
    10-ounce packages frozen raspberries,
    defrosted
½ *cup sugar, or more to taste*
Framboise or kirschwasser to taste
    (optional)

1. Put the raspberries in the container of a food processor and blend to a fine purée.
2. Line a bowl with a sieve and pour and scrape the puréed berries into the sieve. Push the pulp through the sieve using a rubber spatula or spoon. Push as much pulp through as possible. Discard the seeds.
3. Add sugar to taste and stir to dissolve. Add a little framboise or kirschwasser and serve.
YIELD: About 2 cups.

TO SERVE

8 *meringues*
4 *scoops vanilla ice cream*
2 *cups raspberry sauce*

1. Use 2 meringues for each serving. Place a scoop of ice cream between the 2 meringues, sandwich fashion, but serve the "sandwich" on its side.
2. Spoon equal portions of raspberry sauce over each serving.
YIELD: Four servings.

Preparing the Meringues

The first thing you do is preheat the oven to 200° F.

1. Brush melted butter over the entire surface of a baking sheet. You'll need just a thin coat.

5. Use a hand or electric beater and start beating the whites at a very low speed. It's very important to keep the whites together; you don't want to use too large a bowl.

6. Gradually increase the speed until it's on high. When the whites begin to hold shape, start adding the sugar, 1 tablespoon at a time.

7. Keep adding sugar and beating until the whites have a high gloss. Beat until the meringue will not fall out when you invert the bowl.

Preparing the Raspberry Sauce

To make raspberry sauce, use 3 cups of fresh raspberries or two 10-ounce packages of frozen raspberries.

1. Add them to a food processor.

2. Process until they become a purée, and sweeten to taste.

3. Strain the purée into a bowl. If you do not object to raspberry seeds, eliminate this step.

2. Sprinkle a tablespoon of flour over the baking sheet.

3. Tilt and shake the sheet in four different directions to make sure the flour is evenly distributed.

4. Separate 3 eggs; shift the yolk from half of the shell to the other, or from one hand to the other. Don't break the yolks!

8. Take a pastry bag that's been fitted with a round No. 7 pastry tube. Use a rubber spatula to ladle the meringue into the pastry bag.

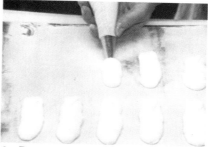

9. By squeezing the pastry bag, carefully shape the meringue into ovals.

10. You can make almost any shape you want, and can become your own sculptor. If you should use a different kind of tube, like a star tube, you can pop out stars and kisses, whatever you like.

4. Put a scoop of very good ice cream on a plate.

5. Press two meringues around the ice cream, one on either side, to make a sandwich.

6. Spoon on the desired amount of raspberry purée and, if you wish, add whipped cream.

Menu Two

Crème Crécy
(CREAM OF CARROT SOUP)

Escalopes de Veau à l'Anglaise
(BREADED VEAL SCALLOPINI)
or
Escalopes de Veau Viennoise
(BREADED VEAL SCALLOPINI
WITH ANCHOVIES, CAPERS AND EGG)

Pommes au Gratin
(POTATOES IN A CREAM AND CHEESE SAUCE)

Salade d'Endives et Betteraves
(BEET AND ENDIVE SALAD)

Granité de Fruits au Cassis
(BERRY ICE WITH CASSIS)

CRÈME CRÉCY
This well-seasoned cream of carrot soup
is delicious served either hot or cold.

Crème Crécy
(CREAM OF CARROT SOUP)

1½ pounds carrots, trimmed, scraped
    and cut into ¼-inch rounds, about
    4 cups
¼ pound potatoes, peeled and cut into
    ¼-inch rounds, about ⅓ cup
1 quarter-pound onion, peeled, cut in
    half, and sliced crosswise, about
    1 cup
2 tablespoons butter
4 cups rich chicken broth
1 cup water
1 bay leaf
Salt to taste, if desired
Freshly ground white pepper to taste
1 cup heavy cream
⅛ teaspoon or less freshly grated
    nutmeg
Pinch of cayenne

1. Prepare the vegetables and set aside.

2. Heat the butter in a large saucepan and add the onion. Cook, stirring often, until wilted. Add the carrots, potatoes, chicken broth, water, bay leaf, salt and pepper. Bring the mixture to the boil, stir, and simmer for 20 minutes.

3. Strain the solids and discard the bay leaf, reserving the liquid.

4. Add the solids to the container of a food processor or food mill and blend or press through to make a fine purée. Gradually add the strained liquid. Pour the mixture into a saucepan or a mixing bowl and add the nutmeg, cayenne and the cream. The soup may be reheated or chilled at this point and served hot or cold.

YIELD: Four servings.

Preparing Crème Crécy

Crécy, a village in France, produced the most famous carrots in the world, and that is why this soup is called *Crème Crécy*.

This is a marvelous soup, with a beautiful color.

1. Prepare 4 cups of carrots cut into ¼-inch rounds.

5. Select a large heavy saucepan or small heavy kettle, and melt 2 tablespoons of butter.

6. When the butter is melted, add the onions. Cook until they're wilted; be sure to stir them so all the pieces are evenly cooked.

7. Add the 4 cups of carrots. You could add an equal volume of cut asparagus, broccoli or green peas for variation.

11. Strain the liquid from all the solids and reserve both. Don't forget to remove the bay leaf; bay leaves do not blend very well.

12. Put all the solids into a food processor and process until it is the consistency of a purée.

13. Stop the processor once in a while and stir down the vegetables with a rubber spatula to ensure that all the solid material gets to the blades. You want to make sure the vegetables become very fine.

16. Add about ⅛ teaspoon of freshly grated nutmeg. Add this at the last minute because if it cooks too long, the flavor is lost.

17. Add a pinch of cayenne pepper if you want, for character.

2. You'll also need ⅓ cup of sliced potatoes; the potatoes will bind together to give the soup a nice texture.

3. Use approximately ¼ pound of potatoes; cut them in half, and then into ¼-inch-thick slices.

4. Finally, prepare a cup of sliced onions.

8. Also add the ⅓ cup of sliced potatoes. These should be stirred constantly.

9. When the vegetables are partially cooked, add 4 cups of a rich chicken broth.

10. Next, 1 cup of water. Bring everything to the boil. Stir once; then simmer for about 20 minutes.

14. Take some of the reserved liquid, and slowly add the vegetable broth to the mixture. You don't

want to add it all, otherwise it will splatter. Set aside about ¼ cup.

15. Now return the carrot purée to the saucepan and add the reserved liquid.

18. Now add a cup of heavy cream; if you prefer, you can add light cream.

19. Stir the entire mixture until it's blended.

As an option, if you want to slightly change the flavor, you can also add some fresh dill. The soup can be served chilled at this point, or you can heat it gradually. This is an ideal soup for all occasions in that it is splendid whether served hot or cold.

Escalopes de Veau à l'Anglaise
(BREADED VEAL SCALLOPINI)

8 *veal scallopini, about 1¼ pounds*
2 *eggs, lightly beaten*
3 *tablespoons cold water*
2 *teaspoons corn, peanut or vegetable oil*
Salt to taste, if desired
Freshly ground pepper to taste
½ *cup flour*
2½ *cups fine, fresh breadcrumbs*
8 *tablespoons corn, peanut or vegetable oil*
4 *tablespoons butter*
4 *thin seeded lemon slices*
4 *small sprigs fresh parsley*

1. Put each scallopini between sheets of clear plastic wrap. Pound lightly with a flat mallet or a heavy skillet or saucepan. Take care not to create holes in the meat.

2. Combine the eggs, water and 2 teaspoons of oil in a flat dish.

3. Put the flour mixed with some salt and pepper and the breadcrumbs in separate flat dishes. Reserve some of the breadcrumbs on the side.

4. Dip the scallopini, one at a time, in the flour to coat all over; shake off excess. Next, dip in the egg mixture to coat all over, and finally in the bread-crumbs. Sprinkle a flat surface with a light coating of the remaining bread-crumbs. As the scallopini are breaded, put them one at a time on this surface and tap lightly with the flat side of a heavy kitchen knife or spatula. This will help the crumbs adhere. If desired, score each scallopini in a diamond pattern with the edge of a knife or spatula.

5. Heat about 2 tablespoons of oil in a large heavy skillet and, when it is quite hot, add 2 of the scallopini. Cook about 2 minutes and then turn them over. Cook about 1 minute, then remove to a serving platter and keep warm.

6. Add 2 more tablespoons of oil to the skillet and cook 2 more pieces. Remove. After cooking 4 pieces you may need to clean the skillet. Continue adding oil and cooking the scallopini, 2 at a time, until they are all cooked.

7. Heat the 4 tablespoons of butter and swirl it in a skillet until it foams. Continue swirling the butter until it starts to brown or becomes hazelnut-colored. Pour the butter over the scallopini. Garnish with the lemon slices and parsley.

YIELD: Four servings.

Escalopes de Veau Viennoise
(BREADED VEAL SCALLOPINI WITH ANCHOVIES, CAPERS AND EGG)

8 *breaded veal scallopini (recipe above)*
2 *tablespoons drained capers*
1 *hard-cooked egg, yolk and white sieved separately*
¼ *cup finely chopped parsley*

1 *peeled lemon*
4 *anchovy fillets*
4 *pitted, unstuffed green olives*
4 *very small parsley sprigs*
4 *tablespoons butter*

BREADED VEAL SCALLOPINI
This variation, Escalopes de Veau Viennoise,
is served with anchovies, olives, capers and egg.

1. Before cooking the veal, prepare the garnishes and arrange them on a platter large enough to hold the scallopini when cooked.

2. On one side of the platter make a small triangle of capers. Surround the top and sides of the triangle with a border of egg white. Surround that with a border of chopped parsley. Surround that with a border of sieved yolk.

3. Cut 4 thin slices from a peeled lemon. Roll 1 flat anchovy fillet into a ring and center it on a lemon slice. Fill the ring with 1 olive. Insert 1 small pars-

ley sprig in the center of each olive. Set aside.

4. Cook the veal as indicated. Arrange the scallopini in the center of the platter.

5. Heat the butter and swirl it in a skillet until it foams. Continue moving the skillet until the butter starts to brown and becomes hazelnut-colored. Pour the butter over the scallopini.

6. Garnish the platter in the center with the anchovy-and-olive-topped lemon slices.

YIELD: Four servings.

47

Preparing the Scallopini

Veal can be pallid or bland if not prepared correctly.

This recipe is simple in preparation and provides a zesty flavor. The breading technique

1. Pound with a pallet or mallet.

2. Make sure that the mallet is flat when it hits the meat.

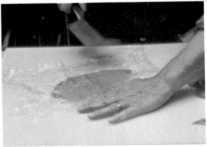

3. If you pound at an angle, you'll break the fibers or make holes in the meat.

Breading Technique

Breading involves 3 dippings or dressings. The first is flour, which should have a little salt and pepper mixed in. The second consists of 2 eggs beaten with 2 teaspoons of oil and 3 tablespoons of water; this mixture should cover the entire piece of meat. The third mixture is breadcrumbs. The breadcrumbs should be finely ground and fresh.

No matter what you're breading—be it fish, fowl or meat—you should always follow this order.

1. When you dip the scallopini in the flour, be sure it is coated well on both sides.

4. Place some breadcrumbs on a flat surface, and transfer the scallopini. Use the flat side of a knife or spatula and gently pat the scallopini to help the crumbs adhere.

you'll learn is the same you would use for preparing chicken, fish or beef.

For this recipe, we'll need 8 veal scallopini. Place the scallopini between 2 sheets of clear plastic wrap or wax paper.

4. Pound it until it is thin and has almost doubled in size.

5. If you don't have a mallet, use a clean, heavy, flat saucepan. Be sure to use the same technique, so that it hits the meat flat.

6. When you're done, the cutlet should be of uniform thickness.

2. Next, the egg mixture. You don't want to have too much egg coating, so you shake the scallopini and let the excess drip off.

3. Finally, put the scallopini in the fine breadcrumb mixture.

5. If you like, you can score the meat for decorative purposes.

6. You can make a diamond pattern by scoring in the opposite direction.

Cooking the Veal

1. Heat 6 tablespoons of oil in a heavy skillet. Then add the veal, 1 piece at a time, to the hot oil.

Note: If you're going to cook more scallopini, you have to change the oil to make sure that the breadcrumbs that remain in the pan don't become burnt and adhere to the scallopini.

Garnishing Options

There are many ways to garnish veal scallopini once they're cooked. The simplest is called *à l'Anglaise*.

1. To prepare *à l'Anglaise*, add 4 tablespoons of butter to a skillet over high heat. Cook it until it turns a hazelnut brown.

2. Keep swirling the butter until it starts to change color. Then pour this over the scallopini.

Garnishing for Veal Viennoise

1. The style we're going to prepare here is *Escalopes de Veau Viennoise*. First, add some capers.

2. Next, a hard-boiled egg white that's been put through a sieve.

3. Then add some finely minced parsley.

50

2. Move the veal in the pan to make sure it doesn't stick; veal tends to shrink a little bit after it's been pounded with a mallet.

3. Veal cooks very quickly and should be turned when it's browned. You don't want it to be too dark; when it's golden brown on both sides, it is done.

Another interesting variant, called veal Holstein, consists of scallopini that have been topped with fried eggs. Flat fillets of anchovies may be placed over the eggs, or garnish with rolled anchovies, olives and parsley.

There's a classic Italian style—*Scaloppine Milanese.* For this variation, you would add grated Parmesan cheese to the breadcrumbs.

4. Spoon on the sieved egg yolk.

5. Finally, add lemon slices from which you have removed the seeds.

6. The finished dish is very festive!

POMMES AU GRATIN
A delicious yet simple dish to prepare:
Potatoes baked in a cream and cheese sauce spiced with nutmeg.

Pommes au Gratin
(P O T A T O E S   I N   A   C R E A M   A N D   C H E E S E   S A U C E)

4 *large potatoes, preferably Idaho, about*
    1½ pounds
Salt to taste, if desired
1 cup milk
½ cup heavy cream
Freshly ground pepper to taste
⅛ teaspoon freshly grated nutmeg
⅔ cup grated cheese, preferably Gruyère,
    although Swiss may be used

1. Put the potatoes in a saucepan and add cold water to cover and salt to taste. Bring to the boil and let simmer for 25 to 30 minutes, or until tender yet firm. Drain and let cool.

2. Preheat the oven to 425° F.

3. Peel the potatoes and dice them into 1-inch pieces. There should be about 4 cups. Put them in a skillet and add the milk, cream, some salt, pepper and the nutmeg. Cook over high heat for about 10 minutes, shaking the skillet occasionally.

4. Stir in ⅓ cup of the cheese and stir until mixed. Spoon the mixture into a baking dish and sprinkle the top with the remaining ⅓ cup of cheese.

5. Place in the oven and bake for 10 minutes. Run briefly under the broiler until nicely glazed.

YIELD: Four servings.

Preparing Pommes au Gratin

Take 4 large Idaho potatoes (about 1½ pounds) and put them in a saucepan or kettle. Add water to cover and salt to taste. Bring to the boil, then simmer for about 25 to 30 minutes. Drain and let them cool. Once they're cool, they become firmer. Peel them, then cut them into slices and dice them until they're about 1 inch thick.

1. Now, put the diced potatoes into a skillet or saucepan.

4. Now add freshly grated nutmeg.

7. Now transfer the potatoes into an au gratin dish. Smooth all the ingredients so they fill the entire pan right up to the edge.

2. Add a cup of milk.

3. Then ½ cup of cream. Add salt and pepper to taste, but not too much salt, as we'll add cheese later that is salty enough.

5. Add about ⅓ cup of finely ground Gruyère cheese. We're going to use another ⅓ cup of cheese for the final garnish.

6. Stir everything until it's mixed, and then put it on the stove and let it simmer for about 10 minutes.

8. Sprinkle the remaining cheese over the dish and place in an oven that's been preheated to 425° F. Bake 10 minutes.

SALADE D'ENDIVES ET BETTERAVES
For a very different salad, combine beets and slices of crisp endive topped with a
creamy vinaigrette dressing. Use chopped, fresh parsley as a garnish.

Salade d'Endives et Betteraves
(BEET AND ENDIVE SALAD)

4 *large endives, about ¾ pound*
4 *to 6 cooked beets, about ½ pound*
  cooked
¼ *teaspoon egg yolk*
Salt to taste, if desired
Freshly ground pepper to taste
¼ *teaspoon prepared mustard, prefer-*
  ably Dijon
1 *tablespoon red wine vinegar*
5 *tablespoons peanut or olive oil, or a*
  blend of both
1 *tablespoon finely chopped parsley*

1. Trim off the ends of the endives. Discard any discolored leaves. Cut each endive in half lengthwise. Cut each in half lengthwise again. Then cut across the pieces 3 or 4 times to make thin strips. There should be about 4 cups.

2. Cut the beets into ¼-inch rounds. There should be about 2 cups.

3. Put the egg yolk in a salad bowl and add the salt, pepper, mustard and vinegar. Start beating with a wire whisk while gradually adding the oil. Stir in the parsley.

4. Add the endives and beets to the bowl and toss. If desired, add more parsley.

YIELD: Four servings.

Preparing Beet and Endive Salad

This is an unusual salad, and a very refreshing one.

1. Take 4 large endives and cut each in half lengthwise.

Salad Dressing

1. For a creamy salad dressing, and one that won't separate when chilled, the trick is to use a small amount of egg yolk.

5. While you're whisking, slowly add the oil.

2. Cut lengthwise again.

3. Then slice across each piece 3 or 4 times for thin strips.

4. Take ½ pound of cooked beets (about 2 cups) and slice thinly. Or slice them julienne, into little match-like sticks.

2. This is quite similar to making mayonnaise, but for this dressing, use only ¼ teaspoon of imported mustard, such as Dijon.

3. Now add a tablespoon of red wine vinegar. You should add the acids to the bowl before you add the oil, so they combine better.

4. Blend them well. Add a little freshly ground pepper and salt, if desired.

6. Beat this vigorously; you want the liquid to become homogenized, very much like a mayonnaise, until it's thick and creamy.

7. Pour the dressing over the salad.

It's a good idea to mix the salad with the dressing in a separate bowl from the one you serve the salad in. As a final garnish, you can add a bit of chopped parsley for color and zest, and a bit more freshly ground black pepper.

GRANITÉ DE FRUITS AU CASSIS
An ice made with a purée of fresh strawberries, lemon and cassis makes a festive and light dessert. Here the berry ice is decorated with peeled slices of orange.

Granité de Fruits au Cassis
(BERRY ICE WITH CASSIS)

2 cups water
1 cup sugar
4 cups fresh strawberries, raspberries, or
    other fresh berries
3 tablespoons lemon juice
1½ cups sirop de cassis, or 1 cup crème
    de cassis, available in wine and
    spirits shops

1. Combine the water and sugar in a saucepan and bring to the boil. Cook over low heat for about 5 minutes. Remove from the heat and let cool. Chill.

2. Rinse the berries and pick over them. Discard the stems and any blemished berries.

3. Add the berries to the container of a food processor and blend to a fine purée. There should be about 2 cups of purée. Add the berries, lemon juice and cassis to the sugar-and-water mixture.

4. Pour the mixture into the container of an electric or hand-cranked freezer and freeze according to the manufacturer's instructions. Serve with more cassis poured over.

YIELD: About 2 quarts.

Preparing Berry Ice

In this version, we'll use orange slices to decorate the berry ice, but it can be served in any number of ways.

1. We'll begin by making a simple syrup. To a saucepan, add 2 cups of water.

2. Then add 1 cup of sugar.

3. Mix it well and stir it until the sugar is dissolved. Bring the mixture to the boil and let it simmer for 5 minutes. Then chill.

7. Add the simple sugar syrup to the purée.

8. Stir well. It must be very, very cold, because it's going to be frozen.

10. Now add 1 cup of *crème de cassis*. If you use cassis syrup instead, use 1½ cups.

4. Put 4 cups of fresh, cleaned strawberries into a food processor and process them until they're a very fine purée.

5. Stop the processor occasionally and stir the berries down. This will yield about 2 cups of purée.

6. Pour the purée into a mixing bowl.

9. Add 3 tablespoons of lemon juice.

The lemon is needed for tartness, as the cassis is very sweet and you want to compensate for that.

11. Stir the mixture very well until all the liquids are blended.

12. Pour this into the container of a hand-cranked or electric freezer.

Almost all ice-cream makers differ, so read the instructions and freeze the berry ice according to what they tell you to do.

63

Menu Three

Palourdes Farcies
(STUFFED CLAMS)

Steak au Poivre
(STEAK WITH CRUSHED PEPPERCORNS)

Pommes Sautées
(SAUTÉED POTATOES)

Salade Mimosa
(TOSSED GREEN SALAD WITH SIEVED EGG)

Mousse au Chocolat
(CHOCOLATE MOUSSE)

PALOURDES FARCIES
Serve baked stuffed clams piping hot from the oven.
Use some parsley sprigs and a scalloped lemon wedge for garnish.

Palourdes Farcies
(STUFFED CLAMS)

32 *littleneck or small cherrystone clams*
2 *cups thinly sliced mushrooms*
½ *cup coarsely chopped shallots*
8 *tablespoons grated Gruyère or Parmesan cheese*
⅓ *cup fine fresh breadcrumbs*
½ *cup finely chopped parsley*
2 *slices bacon, coarsely chopped*
2 *teaspoons finely chopped garlic*
½ *teaspoon dried thyme*
Freshly ground pepper to taste
¼ *teaspoon hot dried red-pepper flakes*
1 *tablespoon butter*
2 *tablespoons olive oil*
2 *tablespoons Ricard or Pernod (optional)*

1. Preheat the oven to 400° F.

2. Open the clams as for clams on the half shell; save the liquid for another use, if desired. Discard the top shell and loosen the clam from the lower shell.

3. In the container of a food processor, combine the mushrooms, shallots, 6 tablespoons of cheese, breadcrumbs, parsley, bacon, garlic, thyme, pepper, red-pepper flakes and butter. Do not add salt, as the clams and cheese are salty. Process until coarsely blended.

4. Using a rubber or metal spatula, smear the top of each clam with equal portions of the mixture, smoothing it over and heaping it slightly on top. Brush the clams with oil and sprinkle with the remaining 2 tablespoons of cheese.

5. Place the clams in the preheated oven and bake for about 10 minutes, or just until they are piping hot. Do not overcook or the clams will toughen.

6. Spoon the Ricard or Pernod over the clams and serve.

YIELD: Four servings.

Opening Clams

To make opening clams quicker, put them in the refrigerator or the freezer (but do not freeze them). The muscles will relax and they will be easy to open.

Use a clam knife, which is straight, rounded at the tip, and sharp on one side. In a bind, you can use a paring knife. Be careful.

1. First, place the clam in the center of your palm, the muscle of the clam facing your thumb.

2. Insert the knife on the side where the shells come together. Apply pressure and lift up the shell.

Preparing the Stuffing

If you're wondering about the difference between littleneck clams and cherrystone clams, the truth of the matter is they're all the same clam. Cherrystones are just large littleneck clams. The larger of the 2 clams here is approaching being a cherrystone.

3. Add an equal amount of stuffing to each clam and smooth it over with a metal or rubber spatula.

4. After they're all stuffed, brush the tops with a little bit of olive oil.

3. Continue working the knife neatly around the inside of the shell.

4. Cut the muscle. Keep lifting the shell or you'll cut the meat of the clam in half. Once you cut the muscle, the clam relaxes.

5. When the clam is fully opened, remove the meat by scraping the underside of the clam away from the shell.

1. To make *Palourdes Farcies* (stuffed clams), put in the container of a food processor 2 cups of thinly sliced mushrooms; ½ cup of coarsely chopped shallots; 6 tablespoons of grated Parmesan or Gruyère cheese; ⅓ cup breadcrumbs; ½ cup of chopped parsley; ½ teaspoon of thyme; ground pepper to taste; ¼ teaspoon of hot red-pepper flakes; 2 slices of bacon; 2 teaspoons of finely chopped garlic and 1 tablespoon of butter.

2. These should all be coarsely processed; it should take no more than 10 seconds to do. Do not add salt to this mixture because the cheese and the clams are both salty.

5. Finally, sprinkle the tops with 2 tablespoons of finely grated Parmesan or Gruyère cheese.

Baking

In a recipe for 4 people, there'll be 8 clams per person, therefore there are 32 clams in all. Place them in an oven preheated to 400° F. and bake about 10 minutes, or until they're just piping hot. If you cook them too long, the clams will become tough.

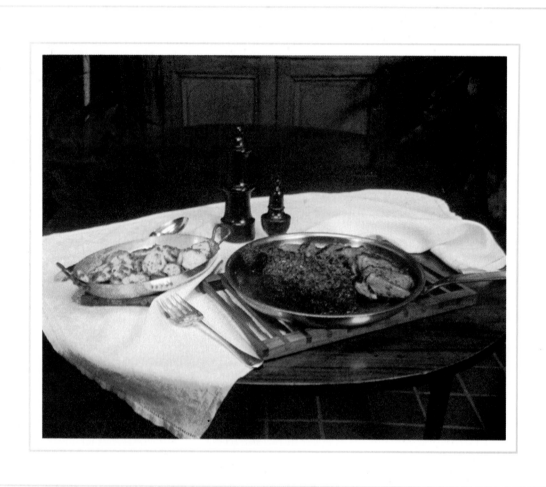

STEAK AU POIVRE
These thick, boneless shell steaks dredged with crushed peppercorns
are ready for serving.
Once done, the meat should be carved and served quickly.

Steak au Poivre
(STEAK WITH CRUSHED PEPPERCORNS)

3 tablespoons whole black peppercorns,
   or 1½ tablespoons store-bought
   coarsely ground peppercorns
2 boneless (New York cut) shell steaks,
   about 3 pounds each and about
   1½ inches thick
1 tablespoon corn, peanut or vegetable
   oil
4 tablespoons butter
¼ cup finely chopped shallots
2 tablespoons cognac
¾ cup dry red wine
2 tablespoons finely chopped parsley

1. If whole peppercorns are used, put them on a flat surface and crush them with the bottom of a flat, clean skillet.

2. Dredge the steaks generously on both sides with the crushed or coarsely ground peppercorns.

3. Heat the oil in a heavy skillet and, when it is quite hot but not smoking, add the steaks. Cook over moderately high heat for about 4 minutes, or until nicely browned. Turn the steaks and cook another 4 to 6 minutes, or until nicely browned on the second side. Turn the steaks on edge so that the fat will cook on that side. Cook about 2 to 4 minutes, then turn and cook the other edge for about 2 to 4 minutes.

4. Return the steaks to one side and continue cooking, turning them occasionally, for about 5 or 6 minutes. Remove the steaks from the skillet to a warm, heat-proof serving platter. Let the meat rest for a minimum of 8 minutes in a warm place. Meanwhile, pour off the fat and any peppercorns left in the skillet.

5. To the skillet, add 1 tablespoon of the butter and the shallots and stir briefly. Add 1 tablespoon of the cognac and ignite it.

6. Add the wine and cook, scraping to dissolve the brown particles that cling to the bottom and sides of the skillet. Cook the wine down until reduced to ¼ cup or slightly less. Add the remaining 3 tablespoons of butter and whirl it around in the sauce.

7. Place the skillet with the steak over a low heat and add 1 tablespoon of cognac. Ignite it.

8. Pour the sauce over the meat. Sprinkle with chopped parsley. Slice the meat on the platter and serve.

YIELD: Four servings.

Preparing the Meat

For *Steak au Poivre*, the cut of meat should be a shell steak.

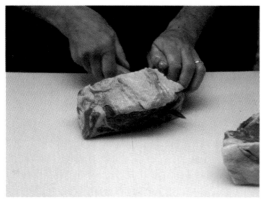

2. Start at the back of the shinbone and cut down.

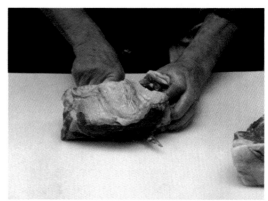

3. Always cut smartly against the bone, following the contours.

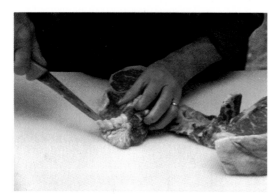

6. Make sure to remove all the fat as well.

7. Cut off the peripheral fat on the top and bottom. The one illustrated here has already been trimmed pretty well.

1. Select a steak that is quite thick. Use the proper knife to bone it: a heavy, thin, sharp, quite pointed boning knife.

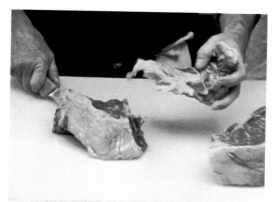

4. Keep cutting until the bone is totally removed.

5. Remove any gristle that remains on the meat. If you have a good butcher, he will have removed the gristle for you.

8. If you want to pound the meat down, use a heavy mallet or the bottom of a flat, heavy skillet.

9. After the steak is boned, it should weigh about 3 pounds. If you're going to serve 4 to 6 people, use 2 of these steaks.

Cooking Steak au Poivre

1. You'll need about 3 tablespoons of whole peppercorns for these 2 steaks. To crack the peppercorns, use the bottom of a skillet.

2. Press down heavily and rock the skillet back and forth until every grain is crushed very, very well.

5. Make sure the peppercorns cover every side of the steak.

6. When you're finished, the exterior of the steak is almost completely black.

9. Stir and shift around and shake the skillet so the steaks don't stick. You're cooking over a moderately high heat.

10. It should take about 4 minutes until the steaks go from dark brown to almost black; then turn the meat over. This should take another 4 to 6 minutes, depending on how well done you like your steak.

74

3. When the peppercorns are cracked, press the steaks down on them.

4. You may add some salt and pat the peppercorns down with your fingers.

7. Select a heavy skillet that is large enough to hold 2 steaks without crowding. Add 1 tablespoon of corn, peanut or vegetable oil, so that it barely coats the skillet.

8. Olive oil is not recommended in this recipe because of flavor. The oil should be hot enough to sear the steaks immediately. Cook the steaks 4 to 6 minutes.

11. It's important to cook the edges of the meat as well. You may have to hold the steak on its edge until it is seared. This should take another 2 to 4 minutes per side.

12. When the steaks are cooked, transfer them to a platter and let them rest. It's important that they sit for 8 to 10 minutes, just as a roast should always rest after it's been taken out of the oven, to allow the juices inside to be redistributed through the meat. You might want to cover them with a sheet of aluminum foil to keep them warm.

Preparing the Sauce

1. To make the sauce, remove all fat and the peppercorns from the pan. You want to do this because some of the peppercorns will be burned.

4. Now add 1 tablespoon of cognac to deglaze.

5. While working, scrape the bottom of the pan all over to make sure that nothing sticks.

8. Now add 3 tablespoons of butter and swirl it around in the pan until it's melted. Be careful the sauce does not boil.

9. Now that the steaks are done, sprinkle them with the remaining cognac and then ignite them.

2. We want to deglaze the skillet. To begin this, add 1 tablespoon of butter to the pan.

3. Add ¼ cup of finely chopped shallots. These should be cooked briefly. Be careful they do not burn; they should just begin to turn golden brown.

6. Add ¾ cup of good dry red wine. It's got to be very dry. Continue scraping to make sure none of the particles stick to the pan.

7. Let the sauce cook down until you have about ¼ cup of the liquid.

10. Add the sauce to the meat; make sure the steaks are fully covered by the sauce.

Just before you serve, sprinkle with parsley. The steaks should be carved and served quickly.

Preparing Pommes Sautées

1. Heat 4 tablespoons of corn, peanut or vegetable oil in the skillet over a very high flame. Add the potato slices and a little salt and pepper to taste.

2. Shake the pan, so the slices don't stick.

Pommes Sautées
(SAUTÉED POTATOES)

4 *large potatoes, preferably Idaho, about*
    1½ pounds
Salt to taste, if desired
¼ cup corn, peanut or vegetable oil
3 tablespoons butter
Freshly ground pepper to taste
1 tablespoon finely chopped parsley

1. Put the potatoes in a saucepan and add cold water to cover and salt to taste. Bring to the boil and let simmer 25 to 30 minutes, or until tender but firm. Drain and let cool, which will make them firmer when sliced and cooked again.

2. Peel the potatoes. Cut them into slices about ⅓ inch thick.

3. Heat the oil in a heavy skillet about 10 inches in diameter. Add the potatoes, and salt and pepper to taste, and cook over high heat for about 1 minute. Shake the skillet and turn the potatoes gently by tossing them or turning them with a spatula.

4. After 5 to 6 minutes, when they start to brown nicely, add 2 tablespoons of butter, salt and pepper. Continue cooking, gently tossing or turning the potatoes and shaking the skillet to brown them evenly. Add 1 more tablespoon of butter and shake the potatoes in the skillet. Sprinkle with parsley and serve.

YIELD: Four servings.

To make *pommes sautées,* use 4 large Idaho potatoes. Simmer them in water for 25 to 30 minutes in their jackets until tender; then peel and cut them into ⅓-inch-thick slices.

Use a heavy skillet: we prefer a skillet of French steel, but you can use any American equivalent.

3. You can stir the potatoes, but if you do, they tend to break up.

4. It's better to toss them in the skillet, if you can learn to do that.

5. In 5 or 6 minutes, when the potatoes start to brown, add 2 tablespoons of butter and continue cooking them. Hold the pan at different angles to make sure the butter is evenly distributed under the potatoes.

6. In about 1 or 2 more minutes, the potatoes will be golden brown all over. Stir in 1 tablespoon of butter, sprinkle with the parsley, and they're ready to serve.

SALADE MIMOSA
This colorful salad of tossed greens sprinkled with chopped egg
and parsley is served with a basic vinaigrette dressing.

Salade Mimosa
(TOSSED GREEN SALAD WITH SIEVED EGG)

1 or 2 firmly packed heads of Boston let-
    tuce
2 teaspoons prepared mustard, prefer-
    ably Dijon
1 tablespoon red wine vinegar
Salt to taste, if desired
Freshly ground pepper to taste
⅓ cup peanut or vegetable oil, or a blend
    of both
1 tablespoon finely chopped shallots
1 hard-cooked egg
2 tablespoons finely chopped parsley

1. Cut the core from the lettuce and
separate the leaves. The leaves may be
left whole, or cut or torn in half or into
smaller pieces. There should be 7 to 8
cups.

2. Put the mustard, vinegar, salt and
pepper in a salad bowl and start stirring
with a wire whisk. Gradually add the oil,
beating rapidly with the whisk. Stir in
the shallots.

3. Put the egg into a sieve and, with
your fingers, press it through into a
bowl.

4. Add the lettuce to the salad bowl
and sprinkle with the egg and parsley.
Toss and serve.

YIELD: Four servings.

Dressing and Egg Garnish

For the *Salade Mimosa*, the dressing we're using is a basic vinaigrette.
(See recipe and instructions, pages 34–35.)

1. Start by pushing 1 hard-cooked
egg through a sieve.

2. Push whatever egg remains
through the sieve with a spatula.

3. After you've tossed the salad,
sprinkle the egg and some finely
chopped parsley over the top. Toss
and serve immediately.

CHOCOLATE MOUSSE
One decorative way to serve chocolate mousse
is in a large serving bowl. Top the mousse with an attractive design
in whipped cream, and dot with candied violets.

Mousse au Chocolat
(CHOCOLATE MOUSSE)

¼ *pound sweet chocolate*
3 *large eggs, separated*
2 *tablespoons cold water*
2 *tablespoons liqueur, such as Grand Marnier, Chartreuse, Amaretto or Mandarine*
1 *cup chilled heavy cream* (see note)
3 *tablespoons sugar*

1. Break the chocolate into squares and put them in a saucepan. Set the saucepan in a skillet and add water around it. Bring the water to the boil. Let stand, stirring occasionally, until the chocolate is melted (heated to 80° F.).

2. Meanwhile, bring another skillet half filled with water to the boil.

3. Put the egg yolks in a saucepan and add the 2 tablespoons of water. Start stirring briskly with a wire whisk. Set the saucepan in the skillet with boiling water and heat the eggs, while beating, for about 30 seconds. Remove the saucepan while beating. Reheat briefly and remove. Add the liqueur. Continue beating, placing the saucepan again in the water and removing it briefly, until the eggs are thickened.

4. Scrape the melted chocolate into the yolk mixture. Stir with a rubber spatula to blend, scraping the sides of the saucepan as you work.

5. Put the cream in a cold mixing bowl and start beating with a wire whisk or electric beater. Beat the cream until stiff. Take care not to overbeat the cream or it will turn to butter. When the cream is almost stiff, beat in 2 tablespoons of the sugar. Continue beating until it is stiff.

6. Scrape half the cream into the chocolate-egg mixture and beat it in using a wire whisk. Add the remaining cream and fold it in.

7. Put the egg whites in a mixing bowl and beat with a wire whisk or electric beater until peaks start to form. Add the remaining 1 tablespoon of sugar and continue beating until stiff.

8. Add the beaten whites to the mousse mixture and fold them in thoroughly.

9. The mousse may be spooned into 4 individual serving dishes, parfait glasses or fluted glasses. Or it may be spooned into a large serving dish. You may also spoon the mousse into a pastry bag outfitted with a round No. 7 pastry tube. Pipe the mousse neatly into the glasses. Chill.

YIELD: Four to six servings.

Note: If you wish to decorate the top of the mousse with whipped cream, increase the cream to 1½ cups. Use 1 cup of the whipped cream to fold into the mousse, the remaining ½ cup for decoration.

Preparing Chocolate Mousse

There are many variations of this dessert; here's the one we like best. For a liqueur for added flavor, we suggest Grand Marnier, or a tangerine-flavored liqueur called Mandarine. Amaretto also goes very well with chocolate.

1. Begin by melting ¼ pound of sweet chocolate in a saucepan that has been set in a large skillet of boiling water. Let stand, stirring occasionally, until the chocolate is thoroughly melted. Then set aside.

2. Next, separate the 3 egg yolks from the whites.

5. Beat them vigorously with a wire whisk.

8. Add 2 tablespoons of a liqueur. Beat all of this until it's very smooth. Continue beating in its water bath until it becomes thick like a gravy custard.

3. Put the yolks in a saucepan and the whites in a separate bowl.

4. Add 2 tablespoons of cold water to the saucepan and start beating the yolks.

6. Place the pan in a skillet of simmering water and continue beating. Don't let the egg yolks get too hot, or they'll start to coagulate and turn into scrambled eggs.

7. Occasionally remove the saucepan from the water, all the while beating vigorously. Be sure the yolk is distributed evenly over the bottom of the pan and does not stick.

9. Now, add the melted chocolate.

10. Mix the egg yolk and chocolate, whisking vigorously with a wire whisk. Set aside.

Preparing Chocolate Mousse (continued)

11. Pour 1½ cups of quite well chilled heavy cream into a mixing bowl. It must be very, very cold.

12. Beat this until it thickens and peaks start to form.

16. To beat the egg whites, use a wire whisk or an electric beater. If you beat the egg whites by hand, try to keep them together.

17. You may want to use a deep bowl to ensure this. Slowly add 1 tablespoon of sugar and continue whisking.

To Serve

We're going to serve the mousse in a bowl, but you can also serve it in crystal, or even plain glasses. Parfait glasses or champagne glasses are also stylish.

13. When it is thick, add 2 tablespoons of sugar and continue beating.

14. This should be whisked until the mixture begins to cling to the whisk. Don't overbeat the cream, or it will turn into butter.

15. Blend 1 cup of the whipped cream into the chocolate by folding them together—do not beat the mixture—and put it aside.

18. Whisk until the egg whites are thick enough to remain in the bowl when you turn it upside down.

19. Add about ⅔ of the egg whites to the chocolate mixture and beat it in with the whisk.

20. Fold in the remaining egg whites, using a rubber spatula. The mousse may seem too thin, but as it is chilled, it will firm up.

1. With the spatula, fold the mousse into a serving bowl. Put the ½ cup of reserved whipped cream in a pastry bag with a star tube.

2. Squeeze the bag while moving the tube up and down in a flowing pattern. Make any design you want.

3. As a final touch, we also add candied violets. They're available in any good confectioner's shop, or in better food stores.

Menu Four

Asperges Vinaigrette
(ASPARAGUS WITH VINAIGRETTE SAUCE)

Saumon Poché
(POACHED SALMON)

Sauce Hollandaise or Mayonnaise

Pommes Persillées
(PARSLEYED POTATOES)

Concombres à l'Aneth
(SAUTÉED CUCUMBERS WITH DILL)
or
Salade de Concombres à la Suédoise
(SWEDISH CUCUMBER SALAD)

Tarte aux Pommes
(FRENCH APPLE TART)

ASPARAGUS VINAIGRETTE
Fresh, in-season asparagus spears served with a vinaigrette sauce
are a perfect accompaniment to any main dish of fish, meat or fowl.

Asperges Vinaigrette
(ASPARAGUS WITH VINAIGRETTE SAUCE)

24 to 32 asparagus spears
Water to cover
Salt to taste, if desired
¾ cup vinaigrette sauce (see recipe,
    pages 34–35)

1. Using a swivel-bladed vegetable peeler, scrape the asparagus spears starting about 1 to 1½ inches from the top of the tips.

2. Place the spears on a flat surface and line up the tips. Using a sharp chef's knife, cut off the spears uniformly at the bottom.

3. Place the spears in a skillet and add cold water to cover. Add salt to taste and bring to a rolling boil. Let simmer for 1 to 3 minutes. The cooking time will depend on the size of the spears and the desired degree of doneness. If you wish the spears *al dente,* so that they remain fairly firm, 1 minute should be sufficient. Drain the spears as soon as they are cooked and run cold water over them for a brief moment to stop the cooking action. Drain quickly.

4. Arrange the spears on a serving dish and spoon the vinaigrette sauce over all or, if preferred, serve the sauce on the side.

YIELD: Four servings.

Preparing Asparagus Vinaigrette

The edible part of asparagus is provided by the spears of very young sprouts, which are very fleshy and tender, and are cut when they are 6 to 9 inches tall. The important thing about cooking asparagus spears is not to let them over-cook. When you buy asparagus, you should select spears of uniform size. That way, they'll cook at the same rate. Buy only crisp-looking, green stalks. Limp stems and spreading tips indicate the asparagus is old, and has lost much of its flavor.

1. You prepare asparagus by scraping the stalks; use a vegetable parer. Start about 1 to 1½ inches from the top, where the outer skin becomes tough.

4. The best way to cook asparagus is to put them into a skillet and distribute them evenly across the bottom.

2. Scrape all the way toward the base of the stem. Rotate until the entire asparagus is peeled.

3. Once they've been scraped, cut the asparagus until they're all of uniform length by cutting off the bottoms.

5. Add cold water until they're barely covered. Add salt to taste, and bring to a rolling boil.

6. Lower the heat and simmer for 1 to 3 minutes. The cooking time will depend on the size of the spears and the desired degree of doneness. If you wish the spears *al dente*, so they remain fairly firm, simmering 1 minute should be enough. If you'd like them more tender, a full 3 minutes will do it. Be careful not to overcook, or the asparagus will turn yellowish and limpid.

7. Drain the spears as soon as they're cooked, and run cold water over them for a brief moment, to stop the cooking action.

8. Arrange the spears on a serving dish and serve with a vinaigrette sauce *(see recipe, pages 34–35).*

SAUMON POCHÉ
Poached fresh salmon is delicious served hot with a hollandaise sauce,
as it is here, or cold with a mayonnaise or sauce gribiche.

Saumon Poché
(P O A C H E D   S A L M O N)

COURT BOUILLON

20 *cups water*
2 *cups dry white wine*
2 *carrots, about ½ pound, trimmed,*
   scraped and cut into ¼-inch rounds
1 *cup coarsely chopped celery*
2 *cups coarsely chopped onion*
¼ *cup coarsely chopped shallots*
   (optional)
⅓ *cup coarsely chopped dill stems*
   (optional)
1 *cup coarsely chopped leeks, green part*
   only (optional)
1 *cup loosely packed parsley sprigs*
2 *bay leaves*
1 *teaspoon dried thyme*
10 *peppercorns*
1 *dried, hot red pepper (optional)*
Salt to taste, if desired

FISH

one 4- *to 8-pound salmon, scaled, fins*
   removed, preferably with the head
   and tail left on and gills removed

1. Fit the rack inside a fish cooker. Combine all the ingredients for the court bouillon in the fish cooker and bring to the boil. Simmer for 20 to 30 minutes and let stand until cool.

2. Cut off a length of cheesecloth about 1 foot longer than the salmon. Lay the cheesecloth on a flat surface and center the fish on the cloth. Roll the fish in the cloth and tie it in 3 or 4 places with string to keep the fish intact as it cooks.

3. Lower the fish into the liquid.

4. Bring the liquid to the boil. There is a Canadian theory that the cooking time for the fish is measured by the thickness of the fish at its midsection. Cook the fish for 10 minutes for each inch of thickness. A fish weighing 4 to 8 pounds should cook in 20 minutes or less. To be on the safe side and not over-cook the fish, let the fish cook in the barely simmering liquid for 15 minutes and then turn off the heat. Let the fish stand in the liquid for an additional 15 minutes.

5. To test for doneness, untie the strings and unwrap the cheesecloth. Tug at the bones along the backbone of the fish where the dorsal fin was removed. If this slips out easily and there are no signs of pink at the base of the small bones, the fish is done. It is best to have fish slightly underdone rather than over-cooked.

6. When the fish is cooked, lift the rack with the fish on it. Let the rack rest on top of the cooker. Scrape away and discard the vegetables on the rack.

7. Carefully transfer the fish to a flat surface. Finish unwrapping the fish and slip it onto a serving dish by lifting up one end of the cheesecloth with both hands.

8. Garnish around the fish with lemon halves and parsley clusters.

9. Serve hot with hollandaise sauce. Or serve cold with plain mayonnaise, or a variation such as cucumber and dill mayonnaise or a *sauce gribiche*.

YIELD: Six to 16 servings, depending on the size of the fish.

Preparing Poached Salmon

A poached salmon is a wonderful dish, provided you get a good, fresh salmon. The first step in making a poached salmon is to prepare a court bouillon.

1. We are going to make ours in a fish poacher. The one we have here is salmon-shaped. It's oval and equipped with a rack.

It should rest on 2 burners for even cooking. Let it cook for 20 to 30 minutes, then let it cool.

4. Now we're ready to cook the fish. When you pick a fresh salmon, look for one with very bright, red, full gills; glossy, sparkling eyes; and with a light gray and lustrous skin. Make sure it will fit in your cooker. It's also best, for the sake of appearance, to leave the head and tail on the fish, but it's also important to remove the gills before you cook it.

5. First of all, trim off all the fins. You can use a pair of scissors.

8. Now wrap the fish in cheesecloth. This helps to preserve the shape of the fish while it cooks. Take a length of cheesecloth about 4 to 6 inches longer than the fish.

9. Place the fish on the cloth and start to tuck the cloth around it. Make sure it's tucked in tightly.

2. Fill the poacher with 20 cups of cold water and replace the rack. Add 2 cups of dry white wine, preferably a Burgundy or other good California wine. Add 2 cups of coarsely chopped onion; 2 cups of carrots that have been trimmed, scraped and cut into ¼-inch rounds; 1 cup coarsely chopped celery; any of the following optional ingredients:

1 cup of coarsely chopped leeks; ¼ cup coarsely chopped shallots; ⅓ cup coarsely chopped dill stems; 1 dried hot pepper. Then 10 parsley sprigs; 2 bay leaves; 1 teaspoon dried thyme; 10 peppercorns; and salt to taste.

It's essential that you make this court bouillon in advance, because it should be thoroughly cooked before you start to cook the fish.

3. Put the lid on the poacher, and put it on top of the stove.

6. Also trim the tail.

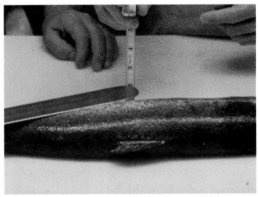

7. Measure the fish: you cook it 10 minutes for each inch of thickness. To be certain the fish is not overcooked, we'll tell you how to test whether or not the fish is done.

10. Take several lengths of twine—4 will do —and tie the cheesecloth around the fish.

11. Put the fish into the poacher. There should be enough liquid so there's about ¾ inch on top of the fish when you put your finger in.

97

Poaching Salmon (continued)

12. Place the lid back on the poacher and bring it to the stove; bring the liquid to a gentle simmer. When cooked, lift up the rack and set it on top of the poacher.

13. Clear the vegetables away from the fish on both sides of the rack, and put them into a bowl.

Alternate Method for Poaching Salmon

1. If you don't have a fish poacher, you might want to cut your salmon in half or into steaks. For steaks, trim the fins off and cut crosswise into 1½-inch-thick pieces.

2. We will use the same court bouillon we used in the poacher and cut the quantity by half.

14. Transfer the fish next to the serving platter. With the belly of the fish facing you, carefully unwrap the cheesecloth, gently placing the fish onto the platter.

15. A simple test for doneness is to pull one of the bones out; if it comes out clean, the fish is cooked. If it's not done, the tip of the bone will be raw and reddish.

3. Put your half salmon or your steaks (called *saumon darne* in French) into either a skillet or large saucepan.

4. You must have enough liquid to cover. Let it simmer about 5 minutes, and no longer.

Sauce Hollandaise

½ pound (16 tablespoons) butter
3 large egg yolks
3 tablespoons cold water
Salt to taste, if desired
Juice of half a lemon
⅛ teaspoon cayenne pepper

1. Put the butter in a glass pint measuring cup and set the cup in a large pan or skillet. Add enough water to come halfway up the cup and bring it to the boil. Turn off the heat and let the butter melt.

2. The melted butter will have 3 layers. There will be a milky white sediment on the bottom, a large layer of clear yellow fat on top of that, and finally a thin, foamy layer on top. The clear yellow fat is clarified butter.

3. Using a spoon or ladle, carefully skim off the top foamy layer.

4. Combine the egg yolks and water in a saucepan. Set the saucepan in a skillet containing water. Bring the water to the simmer. Beat the egg yolks with the 3 tablespoons of cold water, using a wire whisk. Stir vigorously all over the bottom. As you stir, remove the saucepan to keep it from becoming too hot. Alternately return the saucepan to the simmering water and remove it, beating constantly, until the egg yolks start to thicken.

5. When the yolks are richly thickened, remove the saucepan from the skillet, and start adding the clarified butter, using a ladle or carefully pouring it out of the glass measuring cup. Continue adding the clarified butter, leaving the milky sediment at the bottom.

6. When all the fat has been added, add the salt, lemon juice and cayenne. Do not cook further. If the sauce is not to be used immediately, keep it in a warm but not hot place. Never subject a hollandaise to extreme heat or it will separate.

YIELD: About 1¼ cups.

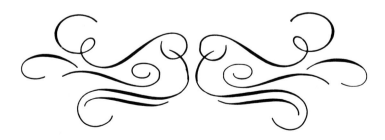

Preparing Hollandaise Sauce

(TO SERVE WITH WARM SALMON)

Clarified Butter

Put 2 sticks of butter in a glass measuring cup.

1. Set the cup with the butter into a pan of water and heat. When the butter melts, it separates into 3 layers.

2. There's a bottom layer that's a milky sediment; there's a very light, white, milky layer on top.

3. The top layer should be skimmed off. The middle layer is clarified butter.

1. Separate 3 eggs (you'll need 3 egg yolks per ½ pound of clarified butter). Put the egg yolks in a saucepan.

2. Add 3 tablespoons of cold water.

3. Put the saucepan into a skillet of boiling water.

4. Whisk the egg yolks and water to blend them well. Be sure the whisk touches all portions of the bottom of the saucepan.

5. When it has the consistency of a custard, you start to add the clarified butter.

6. Remove the saucepan from the skillet of hot water or the eggs will curdle and the butter may burn or separate.

7. Beat vigorously with your whisk and, while you're beating, add a speck of salt, the juice of half a lemon and some cayenne pepper to taste. Beat the ingredients into the sauce, and it is ready to be served. It should be served lukewarm.

Mayonnaise

1 *egg yolk*
1 *tablespoon imported mustard*
1 *tablespoon red wine vinegar*
Salt to taste, if desired
Freshly ground pepper to taste
A few drops of Tabasco sauce
1 *cup corn, peanut, vegetable or olive oil,*
    or a combination of olive and
    another oil

1. Put the egg yolk in a mixing bowl and add the mustard, vinegar, salt, pepper and Tabasco.

2. Start beating with a wire whisk or an electric beater. Gradually add the oil, beating constantly.

YIELD: About 1 cup.

CUCUMBER AND DILL MAYONNAISE

To each cup of mayonnaise, add ¾ cup of seeded cucumber diced into ¼-inch pieces, and 1 tablespoon of freshly chopped dill.

SAUCE GRIBICHE
(AN EGG AND HERB MAYONNAISE)

To each cup of mayonnaise, add 1 hard-cooked egg put through a sieve, 1 teaspoon of finely chopped onion, 2 tablespoons of finely chopped shallots, 1 tablespoon of finely chopped fresh tarragon (or half the amount dried), and 1 tablespoon of finely chopped parsley.

Preparing Mayonnaise

(TO SERVE WITH COLD SALMON)

1. Start with 1 egg yolk.

2. Add a tablespoon of strong, imported mustard.

3. Now add 1 tablespoon of red wine vinegar. It's very important to add these acids before you start adding the oil.

4. Add a dash of Tabasco.

5. Beat with a wire whisk or, alternatively, an electric beater.

6. While you are vigorously beating, add the cup of oil. If you're a beginner, you might want to proceed a little more slowly, adding just a little oil at a time.

Small red-skinned "new" potatoes are the
perfect choice for parsleyed potatoes.

Pommes Persillées
(PARSLEYED POTATOES)

12 *to* 14 *red-skinned "new" potatoes*
Water to cover
Salt to taste, if desired
3 *tablespoons butter*
1 *tablespoon finely chopped parsley*

1. Rinse the potatoes. If you wish to serve them French style, use a paring knife and cut away and discard a wide band of skin around each potato. Leave the remaining skin intact for decorative purposes.

2. Put the potatoes in a saucepan and add cold water to cover, and salt to taste. Bring to the boil and let simmer for 25 to 30 minutes. Do not overcook.

3. Drain the potatoes and then return them to the saucepan. Add the butter and let it melt. Toss the potatoes in it. Serve sprinkled with finely chopped parsley.

YIELD: Four servings.

Cucumbers are a refreshing garden vegetable.
They are an excellent accompaniment to serve with fish.

Concombres à l'Aneth
(SAUTÉED CUCUMBERS WITH DILL)

1 or 2 cucumbers, about 1 pound
2 tablespoons butter
Salt to taste, if desired
Freshly ground pepper to taste
1½ tablespoons finely chopped fresh dill

1. Peel the cucumbers and trim off the ends.

2. Cut the cucumbers into 1½-inch lengths. Cut each piece lengthwise in half and then into quarters. Cut away and discard the soft center with seeds. Trim the ends of each piece so that the slices are more or less oval.

3. Heat the butter in a skillet and add the cucumber. Sprinkle with salt and pepper. Cook, tossing and stirring, so that the pieces cook evenly. Cook for a total of 1½ to 2 minutes; the cut pieces must remain crunchy. Sprinkle with dill and serve with warm salmon.

YIELD: Four servings.

Salade de Concombres à la Suédoise
(SWEDISH CUCUMBER SALAD)

2 fresh, firm, unblemished cucumbers
    (about 1½ pounds)
5 tablespoons white vinegar
1 tablespoon sugar
¼ cup finely chopped parsley or dill

1. Trim off the ends of the cucumbers. Using a swivel-bladed paring knife, peel and discard the cucumber skin.

2. Cut each cucumber in half lengthwise. Scrape away the seeds.

3. Cut each cucumber half into very thin slices. There should be about 4 cups. Put the slices in a bowl.

4. Add the vinegar, sugar and parsley or dill. Toss well. If desired, add up to ¼ more cup of vinegar and another tablespoon of sugar according to taste.

5. Chill until ready to serve as an accompaniment to cold salmon.

YIELD: Four to 6 servings.

TARTE AU POMMES
Here is the baked apple tart, ready for serving.
The top of the tart has become caramelized because the
sprinkled sugar and butter cook together as the tart bakes.

Pâte à Tarte
(SWEET PIE PASTRY)

1½ *cups flour*
Pinch of salt
1 *to 3 teaspoons sugar*
10 *tablespoons cold butter*
1 *egg yolk*
3 *tablespoons ice water (approximately)*

1. Put the flour, salt and sugar into the container of a food processor.

2. Cut the butter into small cubes.

3. Start processing and add the butter pieces, a few at a time. Add the egg yolk, and the water, a tablespoon at a time. Add only enough water so that the dough holds together and can be shaped into a cohesive ball.

4. Gather the dough into a ball and wrap it in wax paper. Refrigerate for at least 30 minues before using.

YIELD: Pastry for a 1-crust pie.

109

Preparing Pie Pastry

We're going to show you how to make a very fast pie pastry, within seconds, using a food processor.

1. Add 1½ cups of flour to the bowl of a food processor. Add a little salt and 1 to 3 teaspoons of sugar. Process the ingredients until they're coarsely blended.

4. While this is going, you start adding water, a tablespoon at a time, through the feed tube.

7. Sprinkle flour on a worktable.

2. Then you cut in 10 tablespoons of cold butter.

3. While these ingredients are being processed, break an egg, and add an egg yolk through the feed tube of the processor.

5. You add only enough water until the pastry starts leaving the sides of the bowl.

6. If you have not added too much water, it will form into a ball.

8. Slowly shape the ball and whatever scraps are left in the work-bowl until it's in the form of a flat ball.

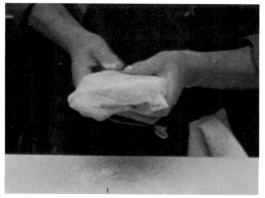

9. Wrap the dough in wax paper and put it in the refrigerator for about ½ hour to let it rest. This will make the dough easier to work with.

Rolling the Dough

When working with pastry, it's best to work with chilled ingredients on a chilled surface. You can work with marble, lucite or wood. We put our board in a freezer in order to chill it briefly.

1. Once you have a cold surface, sprinkle it well with flour.

2. Take a rolling pin that has been wrapped in cloth; the cloth should be lightly floured, since this facilitates the rolling.

6. Continue to roll the dough out from the center to the edge, constantly trying to make as near-perfect a circle as possible.

7. You may want to measure your dough by placing the pan you're going to bake it in over the surface.

11. Press the pastry against the sides of the pan. If the dough should break, it can easily be repaired.

3. Roll the flour from the center out.

4. Keep as much of a circle as possible.

5. As you roll, lightly sprinkle the top surface of the pastry with flour. Turn it over once in a while, for the sake of uniformity.

8. To lift up the pastry, wrap part of it around the rolling pin.

9. Then lift the dough over the pan.

10. The pastry is now over a 10- or 11-inch pie pan, or preferably a quiche pan with a removable bottom.

12. It's almost like a cookie dough because it has so much sugar in it.

13. Roll the rolling pin over the upper rim of the pan; this will get rid of any overhanging pastry.

14. Patch the pastry with any of the scraps that are left over, and you're finished.

Tarte aux Pommes
(FRENCH APPLE TART)

Pastry for a 1-crust pie (see recipe, page
   109)
5 or 6 firm, unblemished apples such as
   Golden Delicious (tart, sweet apples
   such as Granny Smith or McIntosh
   may also be used), about 2¼ pounds
½ cup sugar
2 teaspoons grated fresh lemon rind
2 tablespoons butter, cut into small
   pieces
⅓ cup clear apple jelly or apricot preserves

1. Preheat the oven to 400° F.

2. Roll out the pastry on a cold flat
surface, preferably marble, or a floured
pastry cloth. Use the pastry to line a 10-
inch pie shell, preferably a quiche tin
with a removable bottom.

3. Peel the apples and cut them into
quarters. Cut away and discard the
cores. Trim off and reserve the ends of
the apple quarters. Chop the trimmings.
There should be about ½ cup.

4. Cut the apple quarters into thin,
uniform slices. There should be about 5
cups of sliced apples.

5. Scatter the chopped apple evenly
over the surface of the pie shell.

6. Arrange the apple slices overlapping in concentric circles, starting with
the outer layer and working toward the
center. Or arrange them in any pleasing,
uniform pattern.

7. Sprinkle the apple slices uniformly with the sugar and lemon rind.
Dot with butter.

8. Place the pie tin on a baking
sheet. Place in the preheated oven and
bake for 15 minutes. Reduce the oven
heat to 375° F. Continue baking 25 minutes longer.

9. If you wish to add a glaze, melt
the jelly or preserves over low heat, stirring. Brush the top of the hot tart with
the melted jelly. Serve hot or cold.

YIELD: Six to 8 servings.

Preparing Apple Tarts

Preheat the oven to 400° F. For a perfect apple tart, start with 5 or 6 apples: Use Granny Smith or McIntosh, or Golden Delicious, which is what we're using here.

1. To peel, use a very sharp paring knife; hold it in your right hand while you turn the apple clockwise with your left hand.

2. Cut the apples into quarters.

3. Then cut off the ends with the stems.

4. Cut the center to remove the seeds.

5. Now cut the quarters into thin slices; put any trimmings aside. Save the nice, good-looking slices.

6. To prevent discoloration of the slices, you can put them in a bowl, add a little lemon juice, and toss. The acid in the lemon juice prevents oxidation.

7. Chop a few of the apple slices and the trimmings and scatter them over the bottom of the pastry as evenly as you can.

8. Now arrange the slices in overlapping, concentric circles. Start with the outer layer and work toward the center.

9. Once the inner ring is completed, fill the center with any other broken pieces of apple. Then add more circles of apple slices.

10. Sprinkle 2 teaspoons of freshly grated lemon rind and ½ cup of sugar as uniformly as possible over the top of the apple slices.

11. Dot the tops of the apples with 2 tablespoons of butter that have been cut into small pieces. (The top of the tart will become caramelized as the tart bakes.)

12. Place the tart on a baking sheet and put it in the preheated oven for 15 minutes. Reduce heat to 375° F. and bake another 25 minutes.

DECORATOR TOUCHES
Scalloped lemon wedges, a tomato "rose" or fluted mushrooms
can add interest and color to a wide variety of dishes.

Decorator Touches

There are some who say that the appearance of a finished dish
can affect the final flavor. Although we would never
want to take it that far, there is no question
that simple decorations can add the ultimate touch of elegance.
Here we'll give three decorator touches
that provide just that extra bit of color to set off a dish
along with a few fresh sprigs of parsley.

Sharpening a Knife

You can't do much in the kitchen without a sharp knife.

1. To sharpen, hold the knife in your right hand at about a 20° angle to the whetstone, and slide the blade across the surface of the stone, drawing the knife simultaneously toward your left hand and your body in a smooth, even stroke. Be careful not to put too much pressure on the blade; a light, steady touch is what's needed here.

2. Now flip the knife over in your hand so the blade points away from your left hand. Again, keeping the blade at a 20° angle to the whetstone, guide it both toward your body and away from your left hand.

3. To bring the edge up the side of the blade a bit further, repeat the strokes in either direction, but this time hold the blade almost flat on the stone.

4. To get the tip of the knife as sharp as possible, bring the blade down at a 20° angle so the tip lightly hits the whetstone at the stone's center, and continue sliding it across the stone and away from your body. When you reach the end of the stone, the middle of the blade should be sliding on the stone's surface. Repeat this procedure in the other direction to sharpen the other side of the blade's tip.

Making a Tomato Rose

1. Start by cutting ¾ of the way through the end of a tomato to form a base. Be careful not to slice this base piece from the tomato.

2. Continue cutting a narrow strip about ⅛ inch thick and ½ inch wide, and peel the skin.

3. As you cut, rotate the tomato in your other hand. When the strip is about 4 to 4½ inches long, cut it from the tomato by making a tapered point on the skin.

4. Put the base of the tomato on a flat surface, the flesh side on the inside, and slowly curl the skin around the base.

5. You can facilitate this curling motion by wrapping the skin around your finger and placing it within the flower "bowl."

6. Now cut a second strip of tomato skin and wrap it around your finger.

7. Insert the second set of "petals" into the center of the first, to make the heart of the rose.

8. If there is still more skin, cut a third piece, wrap it around your finger, and insert it into the second tier of petals.

9. When it's all finished, you should have a fairly ornate and beautiful rose garnish.

Scalloping a Lemon

1. Take a whole lemon and cut off the ends.

2. Take a very sharp paring knife and insert it straight down, dead center into the lemon. The blade should penetrate halfway through the lemon, to its core.

3. Very carefully cut through the lemon in a straight line toward yourself to make a single cut, and then withdraw the knife.

4. Now make a second incision at an angle to the first cut. In effect, you will have made a scallop or "tooth."

5. Continue making incisions all the way around the lemon, and when the incisions join, carefully pull the lemon halves apart. *Voilà!* Two scalloped lemon wedges.

Variant: You can use the same technique, but try cutting the "teeth" at an angle.

Fluting a Mushroom

1. Take a very sharp paring knife in one hand and a washed and dried mushroom in the other. Hold the blade of the knife parallel to the tabletop, with the cutting edge facing the mushroom. Grasp the blade between your fingers, just below the handle.

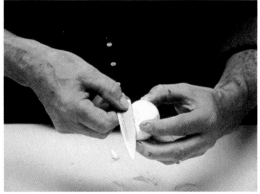

2. The thumb against the blade will act as a guiding pivot. Lightly push the blade forward, letting the weight of the knife press it into the mushroom cap, and pull down in a smooth motion by twisting your wrist. This should cause a strip to be removed.

3. Rotate the mushroom slightly and repeat the previous step. Continue carving uniform strips until the entire top is fluted. This will take a little practice, but it isn't too difficult.

4. When you're finished, squeeze fresh lemon juice over the fluted mushroom cap to prevent discoloration.

Index

124

About the Authors

Craig Claiborne and Pierre Franey are the best-selling cookbook authors and widely respected food writing team for *The New York Times*. Among the books they have written individually and together are *Craig Claiborne's Gourmet Diet, Craig Claiborne's New York Times Cookbook, The 60-Minute Gourmet*, and many of the classic cookbooks that have become the standards in their field.

Both authors make their respective homes in Easthampton, Long Island.